the thing

— *about* —

Fathers

the thing
— *about* —
Fathers

365 Days of Inspiration for
Fathers of All Ages

BLUE SPARROW BOOKS
North Palm Beach, Florida

BLUE
sparrow

Copyright © 2020
Kakadu, LLC
Published by Blue Sparrow

All rights reserved.
No part of this book may be used or reproduced in any
manner whatsoever without permission except in the
case of brief quotations in critical articles or reviews.

The quotes in this book have been drawn from dozens
of sources. They are assumed to be accurate as quoted in
their previously published forms. Although every effort
has been made to verify the quotes and sources, the
Publisher cannot guarantee their perfect accuracy.

For more information, visit:
www.BlueSparrowBooks.org
www.MatthewKelly.com

ISBN: 978-1-63582-186-4 (hardcover)
ISBN: 978-1-63582-220-5 (e-book)

Design by Ashley Wirfel

10   9   8   7   6   5   4   3   2   1

FIRST EDITION

Printed in the United States of America

The **LOVE** of a

Father

is one of life's great

masterpieces.

Introduction

The early evenings of my life as a father have been filled with a most glorious ritual. My two oldest, Walter and Isabel, named it *Special Time* as soon as they could speak. And I am in wholehearted agreement, it is a very special time of day indeed.

After dinner, one-by-one, each of my children make their way down the far end of the house to my office for a few minutes with Daddy. My goals are: to make them feel seen and heard, to remind them that they are loved without exception, and to identify anything that is troubling their little hearts.

More than any other time in my day, it is a time of

listening. As much as 93% of communication in an adult is non-verbal. It may be even higher in children.

So, even though I ask lots of questions, I listen. I try to listen to everything. I listen to what they say and what they don't. I listen to the pause after I ask a question. I listen to their eyes. I listen to the inflection and tone of their questions. I listen to the way they laugh. I listen to how they lie next to me. And I listen to their snuggle, if it is tighter than usual or a little more detached.

"How was your day?" They get used to some of the questions, and their little answers become routine. They answer the first questions with hearts and minds far away.

"How was school today?" I'll ask on a Saturday.

"Good."

"What did you do at school today?" They begin to think about it and realize they didn't go to school today.

"You're so silly, Daddy. I didn't go to school today."

I ask more questions, and with each answer they

reveal a little more of who they are and what is happening in their lives. What would you like to talk about tonight? What's the best thing that happened today? Who did you play with at school today? What are you looking forward to this week/weekend? Do you have any problems? Is anyone being mean to any of your friends? What's the biggest decision you get to make this week? Do you have any questions for me tonight?

You know they have grown up a little when they start asking questions about you and your day. A question as simple as, "How was your day, Daddy?" is enough to let you know they are ready to engage on a whole new level.

They call this part of the ritual *Talking About Their Day*. It is followed by story time and prayers; both are practiced unconventionally. For story time, I ask them to create a couple of characters, and then I make up a short-story based on those characters. Success is when they ask for a sequel the next night.

Prayer is practiced in two parts. What would you like to say to Jesus tonight? What follows defies description. It is beautiful and magical, awe-inspiring, and completely humbling. Their little hearts are so close to God and goodness, and each night, in some way, I realize once again that I have unnecessarily complicated my relationship with God.

The second part of their evening prayer is a simple prayer that has evolved over time. "Goodnight, Jesus. Love you, Jesus. Thank you for a wonderful day, and please keep us happy and safe forever. Amen."

There is one other thing that I make a point to remind my children of each day. "No matter what, no matter when, no matter where, Daddy always loves you. And if you ever have a problem, come and talk to Daddy and he will help you solve your problem." I say it to them over and over again.

"What do you do if you have a problem?" I ask them as they get a little older. "I come and find Daddy and he will fix it," they inevitably say.

"Nope," I reply, and they look at me confused. "Come and talk to Daddy, and he will help you fix it."

We read in the Bible that the delight of God is to be with his sons and daughters. God's delight is the delight of all parents. But only when we embrace the grace to set everything else aside and truly be with them.

Is it easy? No. There are days when I have trouble focusing. Days when I find myself going through the motions during these precious moments. Days when I am tired, or my heart is troubled. We all have days when the requirements of parenting seem over-whelming.

We are all prone to self-absorption. The burdens of fatherhood can be distracting and debilitating at times. Setting everything aside for a few moments requires discipline and momentous effort some days. Make that effort. You deserve those precious moments with your children, and they deserve those precious moments with you. Whatever we think can't wait, usually can.

There is a mantra that dominates the cultural landscape today: "I don't feel heard. I don't feel seen. I don't feel known. I don't feel like I am enough." Let's save our children from this fate by spending time with them in ways that allow them to know, now and forever, that they are seen, heard, loved, known, and valued beyond anything.

Being a father is hard. It's important to know that, because if we expect it to be easy, we will fail. When I think of my own father, there is one enduring realization that I have only come to with the perspective of time: My father is a mystery that will take a whole lifetime for me to unravel, and that unravelling allows me to make sense of so many other things in my life.

It isn't that my father was trying to be a mystery. All fathers are a mystery. Perhaps it's because we can only grasp the mystery of our own father to the extent that we have lived. A four-year-old, a fourteen-year-old, and a forty-four-year-old, each grasp the mystery of their fathers differently. It is unavoidable to some extent, but we can serve our children profoundly, if we simply remain mindful that as fathers we are a mystery that they are trying to unravel. This mindfulness will inevitably lead us to help them with the unravelling.

My own father has been dead for almost twenty

years, and still the unravelling of his mystery continues. It continues each time I catch a glimpse of him in my own children. In those moments it is as if he is winking at me from afar.

The other night, Ralph comes bounding into my office, and I say, "I've been waiting for you for a thousand years, Ralphie!"

"No you haven't," he replies matter-of-factly.

"What do you mean?" I inquire.

"It's impossible," he says.

"What do you mean? Why is it impossible?" I ask trying to catch a glimpse of what's going on inside his little mind.

"You cannot have been waiting for me for a thousand years," he explains.

"Why, not?"

"Because I am only five years old. The most you can have been waiting for me is five years."

"That's pretty clever. How did you work that out?" I asked.

"It's called deductive reasoning, Dad."

I smile, I laugh, I tickle him a little, and cuddle him

tight. "I love you so much, Ralphie," I whisper in his ear."

"I know," he replies.

And that's all I want. For them to know in the depths of their being, and in every moment of every day, that they are loved.

MATTHEW KELLY

January

January 1

My father didn't tell me how to live; he lived, and let me watch him do it.

Clarence Budington Kelland

January 2

If you cannot do great things, do small things in a great way.

Napoleon Hill

January 3

A man's worth is measured by how he parents his children. What he gives them, what he keeps away from them, the lessons he teaches and the lessons he allows them to learn on their own.

Lisa Rogers

January 4

But love isn't just about feeling good. It's about doing what you don't want to do, over and over again, if it needs to be done, for the sake of someone else. Love is really about self-sacrifice.

Meg Meeker

January 5

Children learn to smile from their parents.

Shinichi Suzuki

January 6

I have mixed emotions when I receive my Father's Day gifts. I'm glad my children remember me. I'm disappointed they think I dress like that.

Mike Dugan

January 7

It's never too late to be what you might've been.

George Eliot

January 8

The nature of fatherhood is that you're doing something that you're unqualified to do, and then you become qualified when you do it.

John Green

January 9

The most extraordinary thing in the world is an ordinary man and an ordinary woman and their ordinary children.

G.K. Chesterton

January 10

By the time a man realizes that maybe his father was right, he usually has a son who thinks he's wrong.

Charles Wadsworth

January 11

Fathering is not something perfect men do, but something that perfects the man.

Frank Pittman

January 12

The greatest gift you could give someone is your time. Because when you give your time, you are giving a portion of your life you can't get back.

Anonymous

January 13

If you think you're too small to make a difference,
try sleeping with a mosquito.

Dalai Lama

January 14

Having children is like living in a frat house—
nobody sleeps, everything's broken, and there's a
lot of throwing up.

Ray Romano

January 15

Nothing ever goes away until it teaches us what we need to know.

Pema Chodron

January 16

The challenge of leadership is to be strong, but not rude; be kind, but not weak; be bold, but not bully; be thoughtful, but not lazy; be humble, but not timid; be proud, but not arrogant; have humor, but without folly.

Jim Rohn

January 17

You can't go back and change the beginning, but you can start where you are and change the ending.

C.S. Lewis

January 18

To be trusted is a greater compliment than being loved.

George MacDonald

January 19

Your passion is waiting for your courage to catch up.

Isabelle Lafleche

January 20

I believe that we parents must encourage our children to become educated, so they can get into a good college that we cannot afford.

Dave Barry

January 21

A truly rich man is one whose children run into his arms when his hands are empty.

Ziad K. Abdelnour

January 22

An adventure is only an inconvenience rightly considered. An inconvenience is only an adventure wrongly considered.

G.K. Chesterton

January 23

When I was a boy of 14, my father was so ignorant I could hardly stand to have the old man around. But when I got to be 21, I was astonished at how much the old man had learned in seven years.

Mark Twain

January 24

Be an Encourager: When you encourage others, you boost their self-esteem, enhance their self-confidence, make them work harder, lift their spirits and make them successful in their endeavors. Encouragement goes straight to the heart and is always available. Be an encourager. Always.

Roy T. Bennett

January 25

A good father is one of the most unsung, unpraised, unnoticed, and yet one of the most valuable assets in our society.

Billy Graham

January 26

If today you are a little bit better than you were yesterday, then that's enough.

David A. Bednar

January 27

Make each day your masterpiece.

John Wooden

January 28

Get the little things right. Pay attention to detail. This is a big one in the Teams. It's a core value at my company. In SEAL training you start out by being tested in the pursuit of perfection in what seems like the smallest things. Such as keeping your room spotless. Keeping your knife blade sharp. Taking care of your gear. Watching your swim buddy's back. If we can't get the little things right in life, how can we expect to tackle the real challenges later on.

Brent Gleeson

January 29

My favorite thing about my Dad is that he always makes time to play with me.

Daniel – 10 years old

January 30

Children are a great comfort in your old age—and they help you reach it faster too.

Lionel Kauffman

January 31

My father used to say that it's never too late to do anything you wanted to do. And he said, "You never know what you can accomplish until you try."

Michael Jordan

February

February 1

What's on the other side of fear? Nothing.

Jamie Foxx

February 2

My father gave me the greatest gift anyone could give another person, he believed in me.

Jim Valvano

February 3

Which one of you would hand his son a stone when he asks for a loaf of bread, or a snake when he asks for a fish? If you then, who are wicked, know how to give good gifts to your children, how much more will your Heavenly Father give good things to those who ask Him?

Matthew 7:9-11

February 4

If we have the attitude that it's going to be a great day, it usually is.

Catherine Pulsifier

February 5

Becoming a father increases your capacity for love and your level of patience. It opens up another door in a person—a door which you may not even have known was there.

Kyle MacLachlan

February 6

My dad always used to tell me that sometimes you have to have a massive storm in order to clear the sky.

Apolo Ohno

February 7

You cannot change your destination overnight, but you can change your direction overnight.

Jim Rohn

February 8

A teen shouted at his dad: It's not your job to embarrass me. He replied, "I know." Then smiled and said, "It's one of the perks."

Anonymous

February 9

Years ago we used to play, he used to laugh when I ran away. But when I fell and hurt my knee, he would run to comfort me and the pain would go away.

The Monkees

February 10

As fathers, we have an opportunity to help mold our kids into men and women of character, with morals and values that can't be shaken by the world around them. Of one thing I am certain: we will regret NOT spending enough time with our kids, not the other way around.

Adam LaRoche

February 11

He adopted a role called being a father so that his child would have something mythical and infinitely important: a protector.

Tom Wolfe

February 12

A dad is a person who wants to catch you before you fall, but he instead picks you up and lets you try again.

Anonymous

February 13

Be silly, be honest, be kind.

Ralph Waldo Emerson

February 14

A two-year-old is like having a blender, but you don't have the top for it.

Jerry Seinfeld

February 15

Don't be pushed around by the fears in your mind.
Be led by the dreams in your heart.

Roy T. Bennett

February 16

Becoming a dad is one thing—being a dad is many things.

Steve Chapman

February 17

Everyone has inside them a piece of good news. The good news is you don't know how great you can be! How much you can love! What you can accomplish! And what your potential is.

Anne Frank

February 18

Of all the titles I've been privileged to have, 'Dad' has always been the best.

Ken Norton

February 19

Oh yes, the past can hurt. But the way I see it, you can either run from it or learn from it.

The Lion King

February 20

Every dad, if he takes time out of his busy life to reflect upon his fatherhood, can learn ways to become an even better dad.

Jack Baker

February 21

If I am someone today, it's because of what my dad taught me; that's why I'm a Junior.

Fernando Tatis Jr.

February 22

Having one child makes you a parent. Having two kids makes you a referee.

David Frost

February 23

Don't wish it was easier, wish you were better.
Don't wish for less problems, wish for more skills.
Don't wish for less challenge, wish for more
wisdom.

Jim Rohn

February 24

He opened the jar of pickles when no one else could. He was the only one in the house who wasn't afraid to go into the basement by himself. He cut himself shaving, but no one kissed it or got excited about it. It was understood when it rained, he got the car and brought it around to the door. When anyone was sick, he went out to get the prescription filled. He took lots of pictures . . . but he was never in them.

Erma Bombeck

February 25

Smart people learn from everything and everyone, average people from their experiences, stupid people already have all the answers.

Socrates

February 26

Be a first-rate version of yourself, not a second rate version of someone else.

Judy Garland

February 27

I rescind my early statement, "I could never fall in love with a girl who regularly poops her pants." I hadn't met my daughter yet.

Dax Shephard

February 28

The older a man gets, the more he values everything his dad gave him.

Anonymous

February 29

The father of the righteous will greatly rejoice.

Proverbs 23:24

March

March 1

When I was eight years old, I was called into the principal's office and my father was looking very solemn. And he said, "We gotta go, it's Grandma." We got in the car and I said, "What's wrong with Grandma?" And he said, "Nothing, we're going to the movies."

Sam Rockwell

March 2

The best fathers have the softest, sweetest hearts. In other words, great dads are real marshmallows.

Richelle E. Goodrich

March 3

A small boy becomes a big man through influence of a big man who cares about the small boy.

Anonymous

March 4

A good dad is able to smile when there is little to smile about.

Jake Slope

March 5

Live simply, love generously, care deeply, speak kindly, leave the rest to God.

Ronald Reagan A

March 6

Everything is hard before it is easy.

Goethe

March 7

Children really brighten up a household. They never turn the lights off.

Ralph Bus

March 8

The secret of change is to focus all your energy, not on fighting the old, but on building the new.

Socrates

March 9

You've got to get up every morning with determination if you're going to go to bed with satisfaction.

George Lorimer

March 10

Many a man wishes he were strong enough to tear a telephone book in half—especially if he has a teenage daughter.

Guy Lombardo

March 11

If you are not willing to risk the unusual, you will have to settle for the ordinary.

Jim Rohn

March 12

Jesus answered and said to them, "Amen, amen, I say to you, a son cannot do anything on his own, but only what he sees his father doing; for what he does, his son will do also.

John 5:19

March 13

Those who cannot change their minds cannot
change anything.

George Bernard Shaw

March 14

The greatest gift I ever had came from God; I call him Dad!

John Walter Bratton

March 15

The adventure of life is to learn. The purpose of life is to grow. The nature of life is to change. The challenge of life is to overcome. The essence of life is to care. The opportunity of life is to serve. The secret of life is to dare. The spice of life is to befriend. The beauty of life is to give.

William Arthur Ward

March 16

The father of a daughter is nothing but a high-class hostage. A father turns a stony face to his sons, berates them, shakes his antlers, paws the ground, snorts, runs them off into the underbrush, but when his daughter puts her arm over his shoulder and says, 'Daddy, I need to ask you something,' he is a pat of butter in a hot frying pan.

Garrison Keillor

March 17

Motivation comes from working on things we care about.

Sheryl Sandberg

March 18

To handle yourself, use your head; to handle others, use your heart.

Eleanor Roosevelt

March 19

Be aware of ceiling fans and low door openings
when you're walking around with your kid on your
shoulders. Oh, and one other thing: Get in the habit
of making sure your child sees you smile every
time you see them. Be they 1 month, 1 year, 11 or
21—kids need to know they are people of value in
their father's eyes.

Jim Higley

March 20

Children will quote you correctly only if it is something you wish you hadn't said.

Jesse Andrews

March 21

Father!—To God himself we cannot give a holier name.

William Wordsworth

March 22

If you laugh, you think, and you cry, that's a full day. That's a heck of a day. You do that seven days a week, you're going to have something special.

Jim Valvano

March 23

Every son quotes his father, in words and in deeds.

Terri Guillemets

March 24

The man with six kids will always be happier than the man with six million dollars, because the man with six million dollars always wants more.

William Feather

March 25

Let others lead small lives, but not you. Let others argue over small things, but not you. Let others cry over small hurts, but not you. Let others leave their future in someone else's hands, but not you.

Jim Rohn A

March 26

Life doesn't come with an instruction book—that's why we have fathers.

H. Jackson Browne

March 27

She did not stand alone, but what stood behind
her, the most potent moral force in her life, was the
love of her father.

Harper Lee

March 28

I have just returned from a children's party. I'm
one of the survivors.

Percy French

March 29

The older I get, the smarter my father seems to get.

Tim Russert

March 30

It's the possibility of having a dream come true
that makes life interesting.

Paulo Coelho

March 31

More important than succeeding at work is succeeding with your family.

Meg Meeker

April

April 1

The mark of a great man is one who knows when to set aside the important things in order to accomplish the vital ones.

Brandon Sanderson

April 2

It is amazing how quickly the kids learn to drive a car, yet are unable to understand the lawnmower, snow blower, or vacuum cleaner.

Ben Bergor

April 3

Love is the desire to see the person we love be and become all he or she is capable of being and becoming.

Matthew Kelly

April 4

Just taught my kids about taxes by eating 38% of their ice cream.

Conan O'Brien

April 5

As a father you must have the mindset that being a dad is your most important job.

Mark Merrill

April 6

To love another person is to see the face of God.

Victor Hugo

April 7

You can tell what was the best year of your father's life, because they seem to freeze that clothing style and ride it out.

Jerry Seinfeld

April 8

If we wait until we're ready, we'll be waiting for the rest of our lives.

Lemony Snicket

April 9

I used to believe my father about everything, but then I had children myself and now I see how much stuff you make up just to keep yourself from going crazy.

Brian Andreas

April 10

Listen, there is no way any true man is going to let children live around him in his home and not discipline and teach, fight and mold them until they know all he knows. His goal is to make them better than he is. Being their friend is a distant second to this.

Victor Devlin

April 11

A child enters your home and for the next twenty years makes so much noise you can hardly stand it. The child departs, leaving the house so silent you think you are going mad.

John Andrew Holmes A

April 12

For God so loved the world that he gave his only Son, so that everyone who believes in him might not perish but might have eternal life. For God did not send his Son into the world to condemn the world, but that the world might be saved through him.

John 3:16-17

April 13

Days are expensive. When you spend a day you have one less day to spend. So make sure you spend each one wisely.

Jim Rohn

April 14

My dad's pants kept creeping up on him. By 65, he was just a pair of pants and a head.

Jeff Altman

April 15

If I really want to improve my situation, I can work on the one thing over which I have control—myself.

Stephen Covey

April 16

Heroes may not be braver than anyone else.
They're just braver 5 minutes longer.

Ronald Reagan

April 17

My father was my teacher. But most importantly he was a great dad.

Beau Bridges

April 18

Raising kids is part joy and part guerilla warfare.

Ed Asner

April 19

Remember: What Dad really wants is a nap. Really.

Dave Barry

April 20

Everything you can imagine is real.

Pablo Picasso

April 21

My dad used to say, "You wouldn't worry so much about what people thought about you if you knew how seldom they did."

Phil McGraw

April 22

Do not pray for an easy life, pray for the strength to endure a difficult one.

Bruce Lee

April 23

Character is built little by little, over days, weeks, months, and years, with thousands of small and seemingly insignificant acts of discipline.

Matthew Kelly

April 24

It is better to offer no excuse than a bad one.

George Washington

April 25

Do I want to be a hero to my son? No, I would like to be a very real human being. That's hard enough.

Robert Downey Jr.

April 26

My father believed in toughness, honesty, politeness, and being on time. All very important lessons.

Roger Moore

April 27

Daddies don't just love their children every now and then, it's a love without end.

George Strait

April 28

My father taught me to work; he did not teach me to love it.

Abraham Lincoln

April 29

Coming from a middle-class family my dad wanted his kids to only be limited by their own potential. Maximizing your potential starts by dreaming big and then working hard and giving it your all to achieve those dreams. But he always emphasized that chasing your dreams with humility and integrity was also important. Humility and integrity enable you to leave your community and the world a better place than the one you were born into, which is what delivers true happiness. My parents gave up two decades of hard-earned savings to fund my education, because they believed in me and what I could achieve. Their actions spoke louder than words, and their sacrifice motivated me more than anything else.

Neil Araujo

April 30

My father taught me a good lesson: Don't get too low when things go wrong. And don't get too high when things are good.

Robert Parish

May

May 1

Trust is the glue of life. It's the most essential ingredient in effective communication. It's the foundational principle that holds all relationships.

Stephen Covey

May 2

Dad—a son's first hero, a daughter's first love.

John Walter Bratton

May 3

The just walk in integrity; happy are their children after them!

Proverbs 20:7

May 4

The heart of a father is the masterpiece of nature.

Antoine Francois Prevost

May 5

The same boiling water that softens the potato hardens the egg. It's what you're made of. Not the circumstances.

Anonymous

May 6

I have tried to live my life so that my family would love me and my friends respect me. The others can do whatever they please.

John Wayne

May 7

God works through all things including massive challenges with kids, professional difficulties, tragic fires and deteriorating health.

John O'Leary

May 8

You will ever remember that all the end of study is to make you a good man and a useful citizen. This will ever be the sum total of the advice of your affectionate father.

John Adams

May 9

Fathers, like mothers, are not born. Men grow into fathers, and fathering is a very important stage in their development.

David M. Gottesman

May 10

It is my pleasure that my children are free and happy, and unrestrained by parental tyranny. Love is the chain whereby to bind a child to its parents.

Abraham Lincoln

May 11

My dad is my best friend, my father, and my boss. When I do something that is exciting and he likes it, it feels three times as good as you can imagine.

David Lauren

May 12

My dad, like any coach, has always stressed the fundamentals. He taught me responsibility, accountability, and the importance of hard work.

Steve Young

May 13

Never is a man more of a man than when he is the father of a newborn.

Matthew McConaughey

May 14

My father would lift me high and dance with my mother and me and then spin me around till I fell asleep. Then up the stairs he would carry me and I knew for sure I was loved.

Luther Vandross

May 15

My dad never pushed me, but the big thing is that he helped me by going out in the backyard and playing with me.

Bart Starr

May 16

I cannot think of any need in childhood as strong as the need for a father's protection.

Sigmund Freud

May 17

If you teach your daughter to be good rather than simply happy, she will become both. Teaching your daughter humility is a wonderful gift. And it can be taught only by example.

Meg Meeker

May 18

Me and my dad used to play tag. He'd drive.

Rodney Dangerfield

May 19

I decided in my life that I would do nothing that did not reflect positively on my father's life.

Sidney Poitier

May 20

Healthy families have healthy rules.

James Stenson

May 21

When he smiles, it's as if he's blessing us. We're the parents and should be the ones in control, but he's the little prince, and we feel like we're waiting on him.

Taye Diggs

May 22

I believe that what we become depends on what our fathers teach us at odd moments, when they aren't trying to teach us. We are formed by little scraps of wisdom.

Umberto Eco

May 23

Jesus answered and said to him, "Whoever loves me will keep my word, and my Father will love him, and we will come to him and make our dwelling with him."

John 14:23

May 24

It is easier for a father to have children than for children to have a real father.

Pope John XXIII

May 25

Most of us spend too much time on what is urgent and not enough time on what is important.

Stephen Covey

May 26

It is indeed great news that, despite the challenges, in some ways it is more possible than ever before to have a great career and be a great dad.

Scott Behson

May 27

No one is able to make the female a queen except her father.

Arab Proverb

May 28

When daughters have engaged dads, they benefit from that relationship for a lifetime.

Kevin Leman

May 29

A girl's first true love is her father.

Marisol Santiago

May 30

There will always be a few people who have the courage to love what is untamed inside us. One of those men is my father.

Alison Lohman

May 31

If it wasn't for my sport and my father, I'd probably be a fallen statistic. I'd be dead; I'd be in jail. Luckily, I had a great dad in my life.

Apolo Ohno

June

June 1

When my daughter says, "Daddy I need you!" I wonder if she has any idea that I need her billion times more.

Stanley Behrman

June 2

The more you care, the stronger you can be.

Jim Rohn

June 3

My dad always told me, "I don't care what you do. Just aim to be the best at it. Even if it's the world's best window cleaner."

Bruce Dickinson

June 4

My father . . . He was there when I didn't understand, he was there when I was wrong, he was there when I cried, he was there when I lied. For some reason my dad was always there, when I needed him the most. His love was never ending.

Michael Jordan

June 5

My dad was a remarkable man, a good person, a principled individual, and a man of integrity.

Sidney Poitier

June 6

Be a model, not a critic.

Stephen Covey

June 7

I think a dad has to make his daughter feel that he's genuinely interested in what she's going through.

Harry Connick, Jr.

June 8

One father is more than a hundred schoolmasters.

George Herbert

June 9

I think my mom put it best. She said, "Little girls soften their daddy's hearts."

Paul Walker

June 10

I feel like you don't realize what it means to be
a parent until you become a parent of your own.
Then you feel this tremendous guilt and have this
urge to apologize to your father. You just don't
realize what you're doing to your parents in every
aspect of life.

Max Greenfield

June 11

The two most important days in your life are the day you're born and the day you find out why.

Mark Twain

June 12

Character is not something maintained in children. It is formed.

James Stenson

June 13

When you have a father and a mother who work all their lives so you can have an education and build your body, it's a blessing.

Lou Gehrig

June 14

No father can adequately articulate the experience
of watching his sleeping child—it must be lived.

Meg Meeker

June 15

In my entire life growing up, I've never heard my dad say an unkind word about anyone. My father has always taken the high road in life and to me he's a complete inspiration without being a pushover.

Hugh Panaro

June 16

Children's children are the crown of the elderly,
and the glory of children is their parentage.

Proverbs 17:6

June 17

I have not failed. I've just found 10,000 ways that won't work.

Thomas A. Edison

June 18

A goal is a dream with a deadline.

Napoleon Hill

June 19

The people we surround ourselves with either raise or lower our standards. They either help us to become the-best-version-of-ourselves or encourage us to become lesser versions of ourselves. We become like our friends. No man becomes great on his own.

Matthew Kelly

June 20

Success isn't always about greatness. It's about consistency. Consistent hard work leads to success. Greatness will come.

Dwayne Johnson

June 21

There may be people that have more talent than you, but there's no excuse for anyone to work harder than you.

Derek Jeter

June 22

It's only when you grow up and step back from your father—or leave him for your own home—it's only then that you can measure his greatness and fully appreciate it.

Margaret Truman

June 23

Life isn't about how hard you hit. It's about how hard you can get hit and keep moving forward. It's about how much you can take and keep moving forward.

Sylvester Stallone

June 24

I hope I shall possess firmness and virtue enough to maintain what I consider to be the most enviable of all titles, the character of an honest man.

George Washington

June 25

As soon as my child was born, I immediately wanted to call my parents and just apologize because I never knew how much they loved me.

Ashton Kutcher

June 26

The best thing to try to do is allow your daughter or your son to know that they can come to you for anything.

Jamie Foxx

June 27

From my father I have inherited his clear thinking, reflective nature, and a small portion of his integrity, which I pray will increase over time.

Matthew Kelly

June 28

I'm probably the most uncool guy that they know—
as far as they are concerned anyway—'cause I'm
Dad. I mean dads just aren't cool—especially when
I dance. They don't want me to dance.

Tim McGraw

June 29

A great person is one who never loses the heart he had as a child.

Mencius

June 30

Husbands love your wives as Christ loved the Church and gave himself up for her.

Ephesians 5:25

July

July 1

The best thing you can do, next to rousing the conscience is—not to give him things to think about, but wake things up that are in him.

George MacDonald

July 2

Children develop character by what they see, by what they hear, and by what they are repeatedly led to do.

James Stenson

July 3

True humility is not thinking less of yourself; it is thinking of yourself less.

C.S. Lewis

July 4

Man can banter with his friends and colleagues about whether God exists. But a father looks at his daughter and knows.

Meg Meeker

July 5

We are much more than the jobs we have, the status we attain, and the wealth we accumulate.

John O'Leary

July 6

Happiness and moral duty are inseparably connected.

George Washington

July 7

A man's got to have a code, a creed to live by.

John Wayne

July 8

For a boy to reach adulthood feeling that he knows his father, his father must allow his emotions to be visible—hardly an easy task when most males grow up being either subtly or openly taught that this is not acceptable behavior. A father must teach his son that masculinity and feelings can go hand in hand.

Kyle Pruett

July 9

A daughter needs a dad to be the standard against which she will judge all men.

Gregory E. Langh

July 10

You have to decide what your highest priorities are and have the courage—pleasantly, smilingly, unapologetically, to say 'no' to other things. And the way you do that is by having a bigger 'yes' burning inside, the enemy of the 'best' is often the 'good.'

Stephen Covey

July 11

A father is the one friend upon whom we can always rely. In the hour of need, when all else fails, we remember him upon whose knees we sat when children, and who soothed our sorrows; and even though he may be unable to assist us, his mere presence serves to comfort and strengthen us.

Émile Gaboriau

July 12

The discipline of the LORD, my son, do not spurn; do not disdain his reproof; For whom the LORD loves he reproves, as a father, the son he favors.

Proverbs 3:11-12

July 13

A man never stands as tall as when he kneels to help a child.

Knights of Pythagoras

July 14

Your father . . . He never loses patience, never doubts or complains, but always hopes, and works and waits so cheerfully that one is ashamed to do otherwise before him.

Louisa May Alcott

July 15

Find a song for you and your baby. Make it yours. Dance with your baby to this song every night. Sing it, whether you feel like you sing well or not. Someday, this one song will be your special way of putting your baby to sleep without even having to try.

Josh Misner

July 16

Great fathers don't find fault. Great fathers find solutions.

Reed Markham

July 17

It is not flesh and blood, but the heart which makes us fathers and sons.

Johann Friedrich von Schiller

July 18

Talk to other dads! They are some of your best teachers. Find a place to hang out with other dads. Sharing a brew while doing that is ok, too. In moderation. Your health matters. A lot. You're definitely going to want to stick around for this fatherhood gig.

Darren Mattock

July 19

The value of a loving father has no price.

Anonymous

July 20

A father's words are like a thermostat that sets the temperature in the house.

Paul Lewis

July 21

A father doesn't tell you that he loves you. He shows you.

Dimitri the Stoneheart

July 22

What a father says to his children is not heard by
the world, but it will be heard by posterity.

Jean Paul

July 23

That man is richest whose pleasures are cheapest.

Henry David Thoreau

July 24

You are not going to parent the right way. Nobody does. Parent your way. Ignore the advice you don't like, because if you think the way that somebody parents is crazy, they think the same about you. Don't worry about it. It is your kid, and you are their parent.

Brian S. Marks

July 25

A father's smile has been known to light up a child's entire day.

Susan Gale

July 26

The greatness of a man is not in how much wealth he acquires, but in his integrity and his ability to affect those around him positively.

Bob Marley

July 27

Passion makes idiots of the cleverest men, and makes the biggest idiots clever.

Francois de La Rochefoucauld

July 28

If plan 'A' didn't work, the alphabet has 25 more letters!

Anonymous

July 29

One man practicing sportsmanship is far better than 50 preaching it.

Knute Rockne

July 30

It's not what happens to us, but our response to what happens to us that hurts us.

Stephen Covey

July 31

One's philosophy is not best expressed in words;
it is expressed in the choices one makes and the
choices we make are ultimately our responsibility.

Eleanor Roosevelt

August

August 1

Leadership is a series of behaviors rather than a role for heroes.

Margaret Wheatley

August 2

As a father has compassion on his children, so the LORD has compassion on those who fear him.

Psalm 103:13

August 3

I am endlessly fascinated that playing football is considered a training ground for leadership, but raising children isn't.

Former White House Press Secretary, Dee Dee Myers

August 4

The true measure of a man is how he treats
someone who can do him absolutely no good.

Samuel Johnson

August 5

Life is too short to be little. Man is never so manly as when he feels deeply, acts boldly, and expresses himself with frankness and with fervor.

Benjamin Disraeli

August 6

Men are like steel. When they lose their temper, they lose their worth.

Henri-Frederic Amiel

August 7

If you don't give guidance to your daughter, she'll come up with answers of her own—which means your authority will be replaced by someone else's.

Meg Meeker

August 8

Many people falsely believe that if you want to be holy, you are not allowed to enjoy life . . . Holiness brings us to life. It refines every human ability. Holiness doesn't dampen our emotions; it elevates them. Those who respond to God's call to holiness are the most joyful people in history. They have a richer, more abundant experience of life, and they love more deeply than most people can ever imagine. They enjoy life, all of life.

Matthew Kelly

August 9

Fatherhood is a marathon, not a sprint.

Paul L. Lewis

August 10

Hard times create strong men. Strong men create good times. Good times create weak men. And, weak men create hard times.

G. Michael Hopf

August 11

Tell this to your children: You can tell people's values by what they love, belittle, or ignore.

James Stenson

August 12

Adversity toughens manhood, and the characteristic of the good or the great man is not that he has been exempt from the evils of life, but that he has surmounted them.

Patrick Henry

August 13

The good man is the man who, no matter how morally unworthy he has been, is moving to become better.

John Dewey

August 14

The life of a good man is at the same time the most eloquent lesson of virtue and the most severe reproof of vice.

Samuel Smiles

August 15

The good man does not grieve that other people do not recognize his merits. His only anxiety is lest he should fail to recognize theirs.

Confucius

August 16

The value of a man should be seen in what he gives and not in what he is able to receive.

Albert Einstein

August 17

You can't measure manhood with a tape line around his biceps.

Billy Sunday

August 18

Judge a man by his questions rather than by his answers.

Voltaire

August 19

You can't always choose the path that you walk
in life, but you can always choose the manner in
which you walk it.

John O'Leary

August 20

Every person should be looking to make a unique contribution each and every day.

Tommy Spaulding

August 21

I am not ashamed to say that no man I ever met was my father's equal.

Hedy Lamarr

August 22

On our 6 a.m. walk, my daughter asked where the moon goes each morning. I let her know it's in heaven visiting daddy's freedom.

Ryan Reynolds

August 23

Focus on the best at the expense of the good.

Bob Doll

August 24

You spend time with your family? Good. Because a man who doesn't spend time with his family can never be a real man.

Don Vito Corleone

August 25

The quieter you become, the more you are able to hear.

Rumi

August 26

At some time in your life, you probably had someone believe in you when you didn't believe in yourself.

Stephen Covey

August 27

The greatest deception men suffer is from their own opinions

Leonardo da Vinci

August 28

I've always followed my father's advice: he told me, first to always keep my word and, second, to never insult anybody unintentionally. If I insult you, you can be damn sure I intend to. And, third, he told me not to go around looking for trouble.

John Wayne

August 29

It is a wise father that knows his own child.

William Shakespeare

August 30

Look at my son. Pride isn't the word I'm looking for. There is so much more inside me now. My father wasn't around. I swear that I will be around for you.

Lin Manuel Miranda

August 31

See what love the Father has bestowed on us that
we may be called the children of God. Yet so we are.
The reason the world does not know us is that it
did not know him.

1 John 3:1

September

September 1

The only way I can describe [fatherhood]—it sounds stupid—but at the end of *How the Grinch Stole Christmas,* you know how his heart grows like five times? Everything is full; it's just full all the time.

Matt Damon

September 2

The most effective fathers I've known all seem to be moved by a strategic, far-seeing vision: they see themselves raising adults, not children.

James Stenson

September 3

Because things are not agreeable, that is no reason for being unjust towards God.

Victor Hugo

September 4

If conscience disapproves, the loudest applauses of the world are of little value.

John Adams

September 5

You cannot escape the responsibility of tomorrow by avoiding it today.

Abraham Lincoln

September 6

Embrace everyone and everything that helps you become a-better-version-of-yourself and you will live a life uncommon.

Matthew Kelly

September 7

The quickest way for a parent to get a child's
attention is to sit down and look comfortable.

Lane Olinghouse

September 8

Never ring the bell. In SEAL training, when you quit, you are forced to ring the bell in front of your classmates. The twenty-three of us in my class that graduated never considered quitting. Ever. Yes, of course in life there are things we should start doing and things we should stop doing. But that's not what I am talking about. Whether my sons have made a commitment to a team, set a specific goal or working towards completing their chores, I want them to understand that quitting should never be an option. Do things right, the first time, every time. And never be out of the fight.

Brent Gleeson

September 9

Speaking to the heart is a great encouragement to men who want to be better husbands and fathers. It is both a practical job description of fatherhood—showing how fathers build strength in their children—and an inspiring call to family leadership.

James Stenson

September 10

The greatest mark of a father is how he treats his children when no one is looking.

Dan Pearce

September 11

The imprint of a father remains forever on the life of the child.

Roy Lessin

September 12

When a father speaks, may his children hear the
love in his voice above all else.

Anonymous

September 13

We can do anything we want to if we stick to it long enough.

Helen Keller

September 14

Between stimulus and response there is a space. In that space is our power to choose our response. In our response lies our growth and our freedom.

Viktor Frankl

September 15

I feel like the success of parenthood is feeling like I failed all day today, but I get to wake up tomorrow and do it again and hopefully they turn out to be good human beings.

Justin Timberlake

September 16

I've said it before, but it's absolutely true: My mother gave me my drive, but my father gave me my dreams. Thanks to him, I could see a future.

Liza Minnelli

September 17

You are my laughter and the reason people ask me why I'm smiling when I don't even realize I am.

A.R. Asher

September 18

Honor your father and your mother, that you may have a long life in the land the LORD your God is giving you.

Exodus 20:12

September 19

I know now, that it is by loving, and not by being loved, that one can come nearest to the soul of another.

George MacDonald

September 20

Some day you will know that a father is much happier in his children's happiness than in his own. I cannot explain it to you: it is a feeling in your body that spreads gladness through you.

Honoré de Balzac

September 21

It was my father who taught me to value myself.

Dawn French

September 22

I am not a product of my circumstances. I am a product of my decisions.

Stephen Covey

September 23

The power of a dad in a daughter's life is unmatched.

Justin Ricklefs

September 24

When you teach your son, you teach your son's son.

The Talmud

September 25

Impossible is just an opinion.

Paulo Coelho

September 26

When I was a little kid, the grandfather of a good friend passed away, and I first realized my grandparents wouldn't be around forever. Noticing my sadness, my grandfather asked me to fill a big bowl of water. He told me to make two fists and slowly put them in the bowl, and then asked me to stay there for five minutes. Then, he instructed me to slowly take my fists out of the bowl without spilling any water. "Do you see the big hole left behind when your hands came out?" he asked. Of course, there was no hole, and the water had covered any indication that my hands had ever been there. My grandfather stated simply, "As much as I love you, and you love me, that is how life will carry on once I am gone."

Anthony Goonetilleke

September 27

My favorite thing about my dad is how forgiving
and loving he is. He is just an overall unbelievably
amazing father.

Andrew – 13 years old

September 28

I would rather be the daddy of a romping, roguish crew, of a bright-eyed chubby laddie and a little girl or two, than the monarch of a nation, in his high and lofty seat, taking empty adoration from the subjects at his feet.

Edgar A. Guest

September 29

Nothing is stronger than a broken man rebuilding himself.

Anonymous

September 30

It's not what happens to you but how you react to it that matters.

Epictetus

October

October 1

My [father] told me, "No matter what you do in life, ALWAYS give it everything you have and no matter what happens, I'll still be proud of you."

Max Aaron

October 2

Fathers, do not provoke your children to anger, but bring them up with the training and instruction of the Lord.

Ephesians 6:4

October 3

If there is any immortality to be had among us human beings, it is certainly only in the love that we leave behind. Fathers, like mine, don't ever die.

Leo Buscaglia

October 4

From the time the doctor placed you in my arms, I knew I'd meet death before I'd let you meet harm.

Will Smith

October 5

Lately all my friends are worried that they're turning into their fathers. I'm worried that I'm not.

Dan Zevin

October 6

When I come home, my daughter will run to the door and give me a big hug, and everything that's happened that day just melts away.

Hugh Jackman

October 7

Happiness is not something readymade. It comes from your own actions.

Dalai Lama XIV

October 8

As a leader, you don't have to choose between love and results—rather, strive for love-driven results.

Tommy Spaulding

October 9

My dad just imprinted in my mind from a very young age that you always do what you say you're gonna do when you say you're gonna do it.

Bob Corker

October 10

My father taught me that the only way you can make good at anything is to practice, and then practice some more.

Pete Rose

October 11

My dad always said, "We're the average of the people we spend time with."

Adam Callinan

October 12

Dads are most ordinary men turned into heroes.

Pam Brown

October 13

Never give up on a dream just because of the time it will take to accomplish it. The time will pass anyway.

Earl Nightingale

October 14

The most important thing a father can do for his children is to love their mother.

Theodore Hesburgh

October 15

The world is changed by your example, not by your opinion.

Paulo Coelho

October 16

Yesterday I was clever, so I wanted to change the world. Today I am wise, so I am changing myself.

Rumi

October 17

All we can do is the best we can do.

David Axelrod

October 18

Falling down is how we grow. Staying down is how we die.

Brian Vaszily

October 19

Whatever you are, be a good one.

Abraham Lincoln

October 20

Be the change you want to see in the world.

Mahatma Gandhi

October 21

You must do the kind of things you think you cannot do.

Eleanor Roosevelt

October 22

The quality of a father can be seen in the goals, dreams and aspirations he sets not only for himself, but for his family.

Reed Markham

October 23

Try not to become a man of success, but rather become a man of value.

Albert Einstein

October 24

I'm very at ease and I like it. I never thought I
would be such a family-oriented guy; I didn't
think that was part of my makeup. But somebody
said that as you get older you become the person
you always should have been, and I feel that's
happening to me. I'm rather surprised at who I am,
because I'm actually like my dad!

David Bowie

October 25

What can you do to promote world peace? Go home and love your family.

Mother Teresa

October 26

Don't be afraid to give up the good to go for the great.

John D. Rockefeller

October 27

Let your life be guided by greatness.

Matthew Kelly

October 28

You can do anything you set your mind to.

Benjamin Franklin

October 29

When my father didn't have my hand, he had my back.

Linda Poindexter

October 30

If you believe it'll work out, you'll see opportunities. If you don't believe it'll work out, you'll see obstacles.

Wayne Dyer

October 31

To live in hearts we leave behind is not to die.

Thomas Campbell

November

November 1

Learn to light a candle in the darkest moments of someone's life. Be the light that helps others see; it is what gives life its deepest significance.

Roy T. Bennett

November 2

Keep your face always toward the sunshine and shadows will fall behind you.

Walt Whitman

November 3

Sometimes the poorest man leaves his children the richest inheritance.

Ruth E. Renkel

November 4

A son may outgrow a father's lap, but never his heart.

Anonymous

November 5

Becoming a father is a challenge to any man's psyche and there is a fundamental reorganization that you cannot avoid when you begin this journey. Sharing the journey with other dads makes a world of difference.

Bruce Linton

November 6

The best way to predict your future is to create it.

Abraham Lincoln

November 7

There is some good in this world, and it's worth fighting for.

J.R.R. Tolkien

November 8

As my dad said, you have an obligation to leave the world better than how you found it. And he also reminded us to be givers in this life, and not takers.

Phil Crane

November 9

I choose to make the rest of my life, the best of my life.

Louise Hay

November 10

Your job as a father, your mission in life, is to raise your children to form generosity and character so deeply within them as to direct the course of their lives to greatness. This is what a great father does.

James Stenson

November 11

I have nothing to offer but blood, toil, tears and sweat.

Winston Churchill

November 12

Real love is gritty. It sweats and waits, it causes
you to hold your tongue when you want to scream
obscenities in anger, and it causes many men to
accomplish extraordinary feats.

Meg Meeker

November 13

Whenever I need advice or someone to just listen, Dad is always the man. The confidence he has in me is terrifying and encouraging all at the same time.

Asha Patrick

November 14

You're off to Great Places! Today is your day! Your mountain is waiting, so . . . get on your way!

Dr. Seuss

November 15

Life is either a daring adventure or nothing at all.

Helen Keller

November 16

At the end of the day we can endure much more
than we think we can.

Frida Kahlo

November 17

Do all the good you can,
By all the means you can,
In all the ways you can,
In all the places you can,
At all the times you can,
To all the people you can,
As long as ever you can.

John Wesley

November 18

He always says something like, "Go out there and have some fun. Trust that the Lord has a plan, so go give it your all."

Paige McPherson

November 19

The greatest leader is not necessarily the one who does the greatest things. He is the one that gets the people to do the greatest things.

Ronald Reagan

November 20

Success is nothing more than a few simple disciplines, practiced every day.

Jim Rohn

November 21

Be a dreamer. If you don't know how to dream, you're dead.

Jim Valvano

November 22

Going in one more round when you don't think you can. That's what makes all the difference in your life.

Sylvester Stallone

November 23

When I was a kid, I used to imagine animals running under my bed. I told my dad, and he solved the problem quickly. He cut the legs off the bed.

Lou Brock

November 24

To touch the soul of another human being is to walk on holy ground.

Stephen Covey

November 25

Our greatest glory is not in falling, but rising every time we fall.

Confucius

November 26

I have been loved . . . and that is no small thing.

Matthew Kelly

November 27

At the beginning of your daughter's life, she will feel your love. At the end of her life, you will be on her mind. And what happens in between is up to you. Love her extraordinarily. This is the heart of great fathering.

Meg Meeker

November 28

Character is what children long to see in their parents. It's what children unconsciously imitate in their parents' lives.

James Stenson

November 29

There will be times, times in the middle of the night, while holding your crying child, that you will think I CAN'T DO THIS! Just remember— YOU CAN DO THIS. And you know what, you can do this better than anything you have ever done before. Be proud, be loving —BE DAD!

Chris Nichols

November 30

It's not easy, but it is worth it. You don't have to enjoy every second, but try to enjoy the great moments. And don't just tell your kids you love them every day, show them.

Aaron Gouevia

December

December 1

I realized being a father is the greatest job I have ever had and the greatest job I will ever have.

Dwayne Johnson

December 2

A father is neither an anchor to hold us back, nor a sail to take us there, but a guiding light whose love shows us the way.

Anonymous

December 3

Fatherhood is the greatest thing that could ever happen. You can't explain it until it happens; it's like telling somebody what water feels like before they've ever swam in it.

Michael Bublé

December 4

As a leader, its a major responsibility on your shoulders to practice the behavior you want others to follow.

Himanshu Bhatia

December 5

The real man smiles in trouble, gathers strength from distress, and grows brave by reflection.

Thomas Paine

December 6

The way of a superior man is three-fold: virtuous, he is free from anxieties; wise, he is free from perplexities; bold, he is free from fear.

Confucius

December 7

There is nothing noble being superior to your fellow man; true nobility is being superior to your former self.

Winston Churchill

December 8

Train the young in the way they should go; even when old, they will not swerve from it.

Proverbs 22:6

December 9

There is nothing wrong with being afraid—but there is nothing more wrong than allowing that to be your master.

Bobby Darin

December 10

Happiness, not in another place but this place . . .
not for another hour, but this hour.

Walt Whitman

December 11

Even if I knew that tomorrow the world would go to pieces, I would still plant my apple tree.

Martin Luther King Jr.

December 12

Have greatness of heart. It is the capacity and desire to surpass ourselves, to endure or overcome anything for the sake of somebody else's welfare and happiness.

James Stenson

December 13

To accomplish great things we must not only act but also dream, not only plan but also believe.

Anatole France

December 14

As an educator, I've seen the positive influence that fathers have on their children.

Nicoline Ambe

December 15

There is one rule, above all others, for being a man.
Whatever comes, face it on your feet.

Larissa Ione

December 16

A man knows his limits, but a real man can overcome them.

Travis Martin

December 17

Great hopes make great men.

Thomas Fuller

December 18

Pursuing success is important, but eventually the day comes when we realize the most important things in life were already within us.

John O'Leary

December 19

I'm making life decisions based not on what I want but who I am and who I can serve.

Tommy Spaulding

December 20

Treat a person as they are and they will remain as they are. Treat them as they could and should be and they will become as they can and should be.

Stephen Covey

December 21

Life is about love. It's about whom you love and whom you hurt. Life's about how you love yourself and how you hurt yourself. Life's about how you love and hurt the people close to you. Life is about how you love and hurt the people who just cross your path for a moment. Life is about love.

Matthew Kelly

December 22

Tomorrow is promised to no one.

Clint Eastwood

December 23

Nothing gives me greater joy than to hear that my children are walking in the truth.

3 John 1:4

December 24

Tomorrow is the most important thing in life. It comes into us at midnight very clean. It's perfect when it arrives and it puts itself in our hands. It hopes we've learned from yesterday.

John Wayne

December 25

When I was a young kid, my dad, a man of few words, told my brother and me, "Boys, Christmas is about Jesus." I thought about what he said, and I began asking the Christmas questions. I've been asking them ever since. I love the answers I've found.

Max Lucado

December 26

The longer I live, the more I read, the more
patiently I think, and the more anxiously I inquire,
the less I seem to know. . . Do justly. Love mercy.
Walk humbly. This is enough.

John Adams

December 27

I have learned that to be with those I like is enough.

Walt Whitman

December 28

Continuous effort—not strength or intelligence—is the key to unlocking our potential.

Winston Churchill

December 29

"And I will be a father to you, and you shall be sons and daughters to Me," says the Lord Almighty.

2 Corinthians 8:18

December 30

If it changes your life, let it. Nobody said it'd be easy, they just promised it would be worth it.

Dr. Suess

December 31

He will turn the hearts of the fathers back to their children and the hearts of the children to their fathers.

Malachi 4:6

Allow Motherhood TO TRANSFORM YOU EACH DAY INTO A-BETTER-VERSION-OF-YOURSELF.

ORDER YOUR COPY TODAY!

the thing about Mothers

365 Days of Inspiration for Mothers of All Ages

MATTHEW KELLY

ARE YOU READY TO HAVE
A **POWERFUL**
Spiritual Encounter?

ORDER
YOUR COPY
TODAY!

A PRACTICAL GUIDE TO
LIFE'S ESSENTIAL DAILY HABIT

I Heard
GOD
Laugh

NEW YORK TIMES BESTSELLING AUTHOR
MATTHEW KELLY

"*I am so excited for you!*

This book changed my life. If you only buy one book
this year ... get yourself a copy of *Ask Him!*"

- MATTHEW KELLY

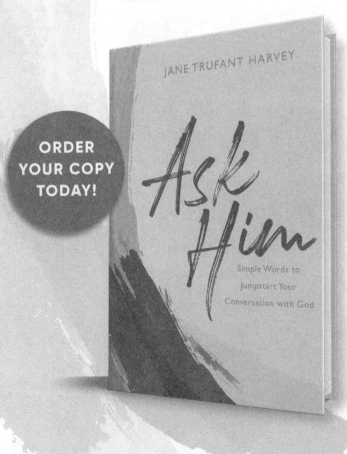

ORDER
YOUR COPY
TODAY!

JANE TRUFANT HARVEY

Ask Him

Simple Words to
Jumpstart Your
Conversation with God

Who you become is infinitely more important
than what you do, or what you have.

Are you ready to meet
the-best-version-of-yourself?

ORDER
YOUR COPY
TODAY!